⌶REP
Birmingham Repertory Theatre

Birmingham Repertory
Theatre Company present

The Gift
by Roy Williams

First performance
The Door
Birmingham Repertory Theatre
on **25 May 2000**

Providing Theatre for Birmingham

EUROPEAN COMMUNITY

European Regional
Development Fund

The Gift

By Roy Williams

Cast

Heather
Doreene Blackstock

Bernice
Claire Benedict

Clarkey
Nicholas Beveney

Janet
Jax Williams

Director
Annie Castledine

Designer
Liz Cooke

Lighting Designer
Nick Beadle

Music
Timothy Sutton

Dialect Coach
Charmian Hoare

Stage Manager
Niki Ewen

Deputy Stage Manager
Ruth Morgan

Assistant Stage Manager
Emma Bleaney

Biographies

Heather
Doreene Blackstock

Training: Coventry Centre for the Performing Arts

For Birmingham Repertory Theatre Company: Bucker & Nanny in *Devil Going to Dance*

Theatre: Deborah in *Casualties* (Soho Theatre Company); Sister Mildred in *Everybody knows all birds have wings* (National Tour); Ayesha in *Downfall* (Contact Theatre, Manchester); Selina in *Girlie Talk* (Belgrade Theatre Studio, Coventry); Zena & Stitches in *Rosie & Jim's Big Theatre Adventure* for Ragdoll Theatre Productions at Oxford Playhouse, National tour including Belfast & Cork; Margaret & Denny in *The Carver Chair* (Contact Theatre, Manchester); Daphine in *Leonora's Dance* for Black Theatre Co-operative, at the Cockpit Theatre, National tour; Del in *Leave Taking* (Belgrade Theatre, Coventry).

TV: *Dalziel & Pascoe* (BBC), *Gimme, Gimme, Gimme* (BBC), *Casualty* (BBC), *The Dark Room* (BBC), *Tom Jones* (BBC), *Common as Muck* (BBC), *London Bridge* (CARLTON), *The Bill* (CARLTON), *Medics* (GRANADA).

Film: *This Year's Love*

Bernice
Claire Benedict

Training: London Academy of Music and Dramatic Art

For Birmingham Repertory Theatre Company: *Mama Decemba*

Theatre: Donna Elvira in *Don Juan*, Maria in *Twelfth Night* (ATC); Nurse in *Romeo and Juliet* (Hull Truck); Lady Macbeth in *Macbeth* (Odyssey Theatre Company); Leonore in *Doctor of Honour* (Cheek By Jowl); Agave in *The Bacchae* (Shared Experience); Titania in *A Midsummer Night's Dream* (English Shakespeare Company); Zenocrate in *Tamburlaine*, Helen of Troy in *The Odyssey*, Eurycleia in *The Odyssey*, Charmian in *Antony and Cleopatra* (RSC); Cornelia in *White Devil* (RNT); Sophie in *Moon on a Rainbow Shawl* for which she won a Time Out Award for Best Actress (Almeida Theatre): title role in *Medea*, Yaloja in *Death and the Kings Horseman* (Royal Exchange, Manchester); Antonio in *The Tempest* (West Yorkshire Playhouse).

TV: *Just So Much A Body Can Take* (BBC); *Dream Team* (Channel 5); *Grange Hill* (BBC); *Call Red* (ITV); *The Bill* (ITV); *Prime Suspect* (Granada); *Text In Time* (BBC).

Radio: *Documents of Identity* (Radio 4); *Those Old Metal Things* (Radio 4); *A Living Legend* (Radio 4); *Raisin in the Sun* (World Service); *Invisible Cities* (Radio 3).

Film: *Felicia's Journey*; *The Fifth Province*; *Sea Sick*.

Clarkey
Nicholas Beveney

Training: Guildford School of Acting

Theatre: *Wicked Games* (West Yorkshire Playhouse); Bottom in *A Midsummer Night's Dream* (Oxford Stage Company); *Big Nose* (Belgrade Theatre, Coventry).

TV: *The Bill* (Thames); *Sharman* (ITV); *Turning World* (Channel 4); *Maisie Raine* (BBC); *Trial and Retribution* (Lyplante); *Respect* (Yorkshire TV); *Pie In The Sky* (SelecTV); Happy Jack in *Lock, Stocks* (SKA Films and Ginger Productions).

Radio: *GosFest92,93* (Choice FM).

Film: *Fifth Element, Basketball Killer.*

Janet
Jax Williams

Training: Jax trained at the Laban Centre in London where she completed a Dance Theatre Performance Arts course.

Theatre credits include: *The Asylum Project* (Polyglot Theatre Company); *Troilus and Cressida* and *Candide* (Royal National Theatre); *The Servant of Two Masters, The Country Wife* and *Sleeping Beauty* (Wolsey Theatre); *The Suppliants* (The Gate Theatre); *Marisol* (Harrogate Theatre); *XS Excess* (Contact Theatre); *King Oedipus* (Leicester Haymarket); *Wicked Yaar, Women of Troy* (Royal National Theatre); *The Amen Corner* (Bristol Old Vic).

TV includes: *Big Bad World* (Carlton); *Casualty* (BBC); *Tracey and Lewis* (Yorkshire Television); *Pummaro* (CineEuropa).

Author
Roy Williams

Training: Rose Bruford College BA (Hons) Theatre Writers' Course, 1997 Carlton Television screenwriter's course.

Theatre: *Night and Day* (Theatre Venture 1996); *Homeboys* (BBC Radio 4, First Bite Young Writers' Festival); *The No-Boys Cricket Club* (Theatre Royal Stratford East, Writers Guild nomination Best New Writer 1996, TAPS nomination Writer of the Year 1996); *Josie's Boys* (Red Ladder Theatre Company, 1996); *Starstruck* – a comedy drama set in sixties Jamaica (Tricycle Theatre 1998 – winner 31st John Whiting Award, winner of the Alfred Fagon Award 1997); *Lift Off* (Royal Court 1999); *Local Boy* (Hampstead Theatre).

In development: *Don't Turn Around* (Channel 4); *Carnival* (BBC Films).

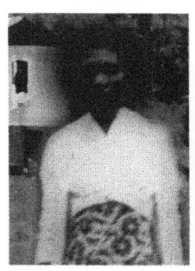

Biographies

Director
Annie Castledine

Annie Castledine was Artistic Director of Derby Playhouse from 1987 to 1990, a historic period for Regional Repertory Theatres. Since then she has worked as a freelance theatre director in theatres all over the country and in Radio and Television.

This year her work includes *Spoonface Steinberg* by Lee Hall, Co-Directed with Marcello Magni and Kathryn Hunter at The New Ambassador's Theatre, and *Marie* by Steve Trafford performed by Elizabeth Mansfield and Timothy Sutton in the first tour by their production company, Visiting Moon Productions.

Her next piece of work will be *The Life and Death of Marilyn Monroe* by Gerlind Reinshagen at the Royal National Theatre Studio in June. In July and August Annie will be directing two pieces for radio, *Autumn Sonata* by Ingmar Bergman for Radio 3 and a new play by Mark Wheatley for Radio 4. In October she will then direct a new play by Bryony Lavery, *Wedding Story,* in The Door.

Designer
Liz Cooke

Training: Slade School of Fine Art and Oxford University.

For Birmingham Repertory Theatre Company: *A Time of Fire*

Recent theatre includes: Lee Hall's *Spoonface Steinberg* (New Ambassadors Theatre and Sheffield Crucible); *Cooking With Elvis* (Live Theatre, Newcastle and Whitehall Theatre, West End); *The Comedy of Errors* (Shakespeare's Globe) and *The Glory of Living* by Rebecca Gilman (Royal Court Upstairs) both directed by Kathryn Hunter; *The Idiot* (West Yorkshire Playhouse and tour); *Volunteers* by Brian Friel (Gate Theatre); *The Promise* and *Arabian Nights: The Tales of Scheherazade* (BAC).

Opera includes: *Carmen, Don Giovanni, La Traviata* (Holland Park Festival); *Tosca* (European Chamber Opera).

Forthcoming work includes: *The Guests* and *Goodbye Kiss* (Orange Tree Theatre, Richmond); *Better* (BAC).

Lighting Designer
Nick Beadle

Recent designs include: *Hosts of Rebecca, Happy End, Song of the Earth, Art, The Devils, The Rose Tattoo, The Rape of the Fair Country, Dick Whittington, Sweeney Todd* and *Threepenny Opera* (Clwyd Theatr Cymru), *China Song* (Clear Day Productions Tour and Plymouth Theatre Royal), *A Busy Day* (Bristol Old Vic), *Vita & Virginia* (Sphinx), *Angels Rave On* (Nottingham), *The Alchemical Wedding, Romeo and Juliet, The Cherry Orchard* and *Racing Demon, The Rehearsal* and *The Double Inconstancy* (Salisbury), *The Life of Galileo, The Resistible Rise of Arturo Ui, The Herbal Bed* and *Arcadia* (Library Theatre), *Killing Time* (National Tour), *Shirley Valentine* (National Tour), *Suzanna Andler* and *Hedda Garbler* (Chichester and Tour), *Vertigo* (Guilford), *Watching the Sand by the Sea* (Derby), *Tosca* (Opera Holland Park) and *The Marriage of Figaro* (English Touring Opera). *Canterbury Tales* (Garrick), *Old Times* (Wyndham's), *From The Mississippi Delta* and *Full Moon* (Young Vic), *Jane Eyre* (Playhouse), *Lady Audley's Secret* and *The Broken Heart* (Lyric Hammersmith), *A Midsummer Night's Dream* and *The Tempest* (City of London Festival), *Gaslight, The Piggy Bank, A Country Girl* and *Marie Lloyd* (Greenwich), *A Better Day* and *Waiting to Inhale* (Theatre Royal Stratford East), *Hymn to Love - Homage to Piaf* (Drill Hall), *Women of Troy* (Royal National Theatre).

Music
Timothy Sutton

Timothy was the assistant conductor of Simon Callow's recent revival of *The Pajama Game* (Birmingham Repertory Theatre, Victoria Palace). He has written three musicals, *Beauty and the Beast* which won Best Musical, Vivian Ellis Prize 1990, *Civilisation,* and *Oak.*

Musical direction includes: *Marat/Sade* (Royal National Theatre), *Hymn to Love* (Mercury Colchester, Drill Hall, Traverse Edinburgh and BBC Radio 3), *Killing Rasputin* (Bridewell Theatre), *China Song* (Plymouth Drum and touring), and *Marie* (Basingstoke, Keswick and touring).

Incidental music includes: *A Fool and His Money...* (Nottingham Playhouse, Birmingham Repertory Theatre).

Timothy works closely with director Annie Castledine and Visiting Moon Productions.

Welcome to The Door

If this is your first time at The Door, we thought we should let you know what you've been missing ...

The Door is the Rep's theatre for new work. Our aim is to present an accessible, entertaining and challenging season of new plays each year; a season that provides a space for a range of contemporary voices; that reflects a diversity of style, subject matter and perspective, and creates a different experience of the theatre every time.

So, by the end of this season, we will have taken you from a roof-top to a corner-shop; from Judea to Jamaica; from Moira Buffini's millennial medieval comedy, SILENCE; to the contemporary curry kitchens of Brum in BALTI KINGS; from one night in an African cave in Charles Mulekwa's drama, A TIME OF FIRE to another of acid childhood recriminations in Tamsin Oglesby's black comedy MY BEST FRIEND.

What's more, our shows are now consistently breaking their box office targets, bringing together younger and older audiences, first time and regular attenders and building an audience for new work made in Birmingham.

New plays for our programme come from a variety of sources. One is the writers' attachment scheme, which this year has been sponsored by Channel 4 Television. This provides an opportunity for writers to explore new ideas and to experiment. Both TERRACOTTA by Jess Walters and Ray Grewal's MY DAD'S CORNER SHOP started life on the scheme as the briefest of outlines and went on to become successful productions in our current season.

Later this year, you can also see the fruits of more work with young writers in our TRANSMISSIONS festival in July. Here are plays of astonishing maturity and wit written by writers as young as 12, with subjects ranging from an epic drama of twins separated by religion, to a comedy about the curse of embarrassing parents. Hard on their heels follows our youth theatre, The Young Rep, who will present their collaboration with playwright Michael Punter on an irreverent reworking of Aristophanes' classic satire THE BIRDS.

Meanwhile, we're now in the process of finalising the next season of work in The Door starting in the Autumn. With your help this new theatre for new work can only go from strength to strength.

We hope to see you there.

Anthony Clark
Associate Artistic Director

My Best Friend

Transmissions

Transmissions is The Rep's training project aimed at nurturing the playwrights of the future. It gives twenty-five young people from across the region the chance to develop their writing skills in a constructive and creative way. Indeed the wealth and diversity of talent among young writers in the region is becoming increasingly apparent as we approach the second Transmissions Festival.

There are currently two groups of young writers involved in Transmissions, one of 11 to 16 year olds and the other of writers between 17 – 25. Since last October both groups have been working with three playwrights, Noel Greig, Carl Miller and Maya Chowdhray. With their help the Transmissions writers have been developing initial ideas into full and complete scripts through a series of workshops and constructive feedback. The scheme also allows participants to meet other young writers in a fun and interactive environment, giving them the support and encouragement needed to expand their interest into an active process with a very definite aim; to see their work performed on stage by professional actors.

In July the writers will be working with professional theatre practitioners – directors, actors, designers – to present a showcase of their work in the form of the Transmissions Festival. The festival will take place over a series of evenings when the works of all the writers will be shown. It is a celebration and demonstration of their work, enabling them to gain an insight into the collaborative process involved in theatre once the initial writing stage is complete.

This is the second Transmissions Festival since the creation of the scheme and the first, held last summer, was a great success. This year promises to be just as exciting, with the writers taking over The Door to show just what they can do!

The Transmissions Festival runs from 6 – 19 July 2000. For more information about the festival or the Transmissions scheme contact Caroline Jester in the Literary Department at The Rep on **0121 245 2000**.

The Young Rep, a company for young people aged between 7 – 19, has been running for just under a year and currently has 100 members who are committed to learning about drama and performance. They have developed a range of performance and production skills from our in-house team, as well as participating in weekly workshops led by professional drama practitioners and directors.

Earlier in the year the company had their first opportunity to perform in The Door. The three working groups created a week of devised and scripted performances, *youngreplive2k*. As well performing, students worked backstage, stage-managing and cueing the performances in accordance with the company's commitment to training students in all areas of the theatre.

In July The Young Rep will be staging its first full-scale performance in The Door. The students will get the opportunity to work with Michael Punter, a playwright who has been specially commissioned to write a new adaptation of *The Birds* by Aristophanes for the company. The students will work closely with Michael and the directing team, exploring the text and developing ideas for performance.

The Birds by Aristophanes
in a new adaptation by Michael Punter
Thur 27 to Sat 29 July, 7.45pm.
Saturday matinee 2.45pm.
The Door

The Young Rep welcomes young people from across the area. If you would like more information either about joining the Young Rep or forthcoming Young Rep productions, please contact the **Education Department on 0121 245 2000**.

Designed to be an holistic experience of the process of writing and producing a new play, a place in the Page to Stage scheme includes:

- Hugely subsidised tickets for the plays in The Door, the equivalent of £3.00 per show.

- Scripts of the plays at cost.

- Workshops: two supporting workshops, the first in school to introduce the plays, and the second at the theatre with the writer and director.

- Afterdarks: discussion with the cast after the show

This package is available for FE, HE and sixth form students as well as Youth and Community groups (16+).

For further information about Page to Stage please contact the **Education department on 0121 245 2000**.

The Gift

by
Roy Williams

Methuen Drama

Published by Methuen Drama

1 3 5 7 9 10 8 6 4 2

First published in Great Britain in 2000 by Methuen Publishing Limited

Copyright © 2000 Roy Williams

Roy Williams has asserted his rights under the Copyright, Designs and
Patents Act, 1988, to be identified as the author of this work

A CIP catalogue record is available from the British Library

ISBN 0 413 75590 8

Typeset by SX Composing DTP, Rayleigh, Essex
Printed and bound in Great Britain by
Cox & Wyman Ltd, Reading, Berkshire

The Gift

Characters

Bernice
Heather
Janet
Clarkey

Setting
Clarendon, Jamaica

Note
Bernice and Heather are both fifteen years old in the first scene and in their late forties thereafter.

Scene One

A graveyard, Clarendon, Jamaica. Afternoon. **Bernice,** *fifteen, comes running on. She looks inside a small grave that hasn't been filled yet.*

Bernice (*whispers*)   She soon come.

She looks around quickly before deciding where to hide. **Heather,** *also fifteen, comes running on. She looks around suspiciously for* **Bernice.** **Heather** *does not notice* **Bernice** *creeping up behind her.* **Bernice** *grabs* **Heather** *from behind.*

Bernice   Slip yu!

Heather   Slip yu back!

Bernice   Yu can't slip mi back.

Heather   Why not?

Bernice   Ca I awready slip yu, game finish Header, mi win.

Heather   It nuh finish.

Bernice   It finish.

Heather   Yu go tell mi we play best outta three.

Bernice   And dis is de third.

Heather   Second, yu so stupid.

Bernice   Third. Don't talk like I fool girl.

Heather   Well don't act like fool.

Bernice   We were playin' slip outside yer house an hour ago, Clarkey was deh remember?

Heather   Dat weren't a go.

Bernice   Shut yer mout'.

Heather   It were not. We were jus' showin' Clarkey how to play de game.

Bernice   An' we did. We played it fer trut', right? Third go, I win.

Heather   Nossir.

Bernice   Fine den. Gwan wid yerself, for de rest a' de day.

Heather   Bernice, is why yu love to moan?

Bernice   Header, is why yu love to cheat?

Heather   I don't cheat, it not my fault yu can't count.

Bernice   I can count!

Heather   Yu don' go school, everybody know dat. Yu can' even read.

Bernice   I can read!

Heather   Yeah like sum fool, like Connie Williams, yu come jus' like she, fall on yer head when she a baby.

Bernice   An' yu tink yu so clever?

Heather   Mi know.

Bernice   Yer fart.

Heather   I get two As for history an' math, Bernice, two! Is how many yu ever get?

Bernice   When yu say yer leavin'?

Heather   Four o'clock.

Bernice   Yu wan' live till den?

Heather   Touch mi I tell mi mudda.

Bernice   Yu tell yer mudda, I go put spell on yu, mek all hair fall out next mornin'.

Heather   Yer fart!

Bernice   Every bit a' it.

Heather   Leave mi alone, right?

Bernice (*laughs*)   Fool. Yu believe mi.

Heather   I never say I believe yu.

Bernice   Yer face do.

Heather   Mi can't wait to get away from yu.

Bernice   I can't wait fer yu to get away from mi.

Heather   Yu mean yu won't miss me.

Bernice   Nope.

Heather   Yu lie.

Bernice   So why yu ask mi?

Heather   Why yu so nasty to mi?

Bernice   Yu nasty to mi.

Heather   Yu will miss mi, won't yu Bernice? I is never go ferget yu Bernice.

Bernice   Yu too lie.

Heather   Mi nuh lie.

Bernice   As soon as yu arrive in England, yu is gonna ferget all about mi. Jus' like everybody else. Everyone ferget 'bout Bernice.

Heather   I won't.

Bernice   Lie!

Heather   I hate yu, yu nuh!

Bernice   Hate yu too.

Heather *bursts into tears.*

Bernice   Oh come on, don't even tink 'bout dat Header Stuart. Jus' no budda. Wat, yu get A in acting as well? Stop it. Yu nuh hear wat mi say, stop it. Yu love to tek joke too far Header! Awright, awright, I go miss yu too, but only a lickle, right?

Heather   Lickle?

Bernice   Awright a lot. Child I go miss yu a lot. Now stop yer cryin'.

Heather (*with great ease*)   Awright den! (*Laughs.*)

Bernice   Yu lickle rass yu!

Heather (*chants*)   Yu say yu love mi, yu say yu love mi . . .

Bernice   Nasty lickle bitch.

Heather   Yu wan' sum advice Bernice, yu wan' be smart like mi, go back to school, mi mudda go school, an' look, two a' we go on a plane, fly to England. Or yu want stay on dis island, and grow stupid?

Bernice   Move from mi.

Heather   Yu wan' cry Bernice.

Bernice   Yu and yer mudda think yu so better than we.

Heather   Because we are.

Bernice   Carry on, gwan like she.

Heather   I will.

Bernice   Let's si how high and mighty she is living in Englan'.

Heather   We go live in a big house, we go have servants. Daddy say in him last letter.

Bernice   Him nuh say dat.

Heather   How yu know?

Bernice   Yu tell mi las' time yu hear from him, him get job working in factory, ware dem mek tele.

Heather   Yes.

Bernice   But now him have enough to have servants?

Heather   Yes.

Bernice   So tell mi summin, how come my mudda's cousin Frankie, who also go England, tell mi mudda dat he bump into yer daddy, deh work in de same place, and cousin Frankie him nuh have no servants.

Heather   Shut yer mout'.

Bernice   Yu tell so much lie. One day yer nose grow so big, it go drop off. I'm glad we stayin' here.

Heather   I go live in Putney.

Bernice   Putney?

Heather   It's in London.

Bernice   Sound like summin yu put between two slices a' bread.

Bernice *takes out a large cigar and lights it.*

Heather   Is ware de hell yu get dat?

Bernice   Mi find it.

Heather   Inside Grandaddy's jacket is ware yu find it. Him favourite cigars dat, yu nuh.

Heather   Give it back.

Bernice   Move.

Heather   It nuh belong to yu.

Bernice   Yu want fight yer cousin Header?

Heather   Keep de stupid cigar, Granddaddy away smell bad anyhow. Mama away mek him smoke outside de house.

Bernice *blows smoke in her face.*

Heather   Move! Let mi have a smoke? (*Takes the cigar.*) I miss him yu nuh Bernice.

Bernice   Who?

Heather   Dadda.

Bernice   How can yu miss 'im, yu only lickle when 'im go, yu can't remember 'im.

Heather   Don't mean I can't miss 'im, ware it say I can't miss 'im? And I do remember 'im, wid his big smile an 'im gold tooth. First ting I do when mi get to Englan', I go give him a big hug yu si. I go hold him, never let go.

Bernice   My turn! (*Snatches the cigar.*)

Heather (*protests*)   Hey!

Bernice   Watch mi now. (*Blows smoke rings.*)

Heather   It's cold. Yu nuh feel cold?

Bernice   We in a grave field.

Heather   Yeah, but dat no reason to feel cold though. Wat was dat?

Bernice   Wat was wat?

Heather   Dat gust a' wind. Yu nuh feel it?

Bernice   Must be de spirits.

Heather   Duppies?

Bernice   Deh all around us.

Heather   Dem dead.

Bernice   Dem tortured spirits Header.

Heather   Yu too lie.

Bernice   Caught between worlds.

Heather   Which worlds?

Bernice   Dis world and de oder life, yu so stupid.

Heather   Yu stupid!

Bernice   Yu afraid?

Heather   No.

Bernice   Yu want talk to dem?

Heather   Shut yer mout' Bernice.

Bernice   I thought yu say yu not afraid.

Heather   I'm not.

Bernice   Come on den.

Heather   Yu can't talk to ghosts!

Bernice   Den yu got nuttin to be afraid of.

Heather   Awright. Gwan den. If yu can.

Bernice   So who yu want to speak to, Grandma? Uncle Sammy? Yer old dog Sparkey?

Heather   How de hell can I speak to a dog?

Bernice   Uncle Sammy den.

Heather   How yu go do this?

Bernice   Watch.

Bernice *kneels beside Sammy's grave. She places her hand on the grave and closes her eyes. She slowly begins to chant.*

Heather (*laughs*)   Come on Bernice, enough is enough. Bernice, Bernice! I don't believe yu. Stop it, I not scared, right? Stop it!

Bernice (*in another voice*)   Header Stuart!

Heather *shrieks.*

Bernice   Yu bin a good girl, Header?

Heather   Stop it Bernice. Yu love to tek joke too far.

Bernice   Bernice? Who dat?

Heather   Uncle Sammy?

Bernice   Yu bin a good girl fer yer mudda, Header?

Heather   Yes, Uncle Sammy.

Bernice   Wat yu doin' wid yerself?

Heather   I going to England, Uncle Sammy. To live. I go si mi daddy.

Bernice   Yer daddy? Him a good man, Header. Mind yu tek care a' him.

Heather   Yes, Uncle Sammy.

Bernice   Yu sure yu bin a good girl, Header?

Heather   Yes.

Bernice   So wa 'appen to mi dog Sparkey?

Heather   Him get sick, Uncle Sammy.

Bernice   Don't lie to mi girl.

Heather   She run into de road, Uncle Sammy, get hit by car. I try to hold on, but she too quick.

Bernice   Yu kill my dog?

Heather   No, Uncle Sammy.

Bernice   When I ask yu to tek care a' her.

Heather   Mi sorry.

Bernice   It awright Heather. It not yer fault yu kill mi dog. Come outta deh Sparkey.

Heather   Bernice can yu hear mi girl?

Bernice   Sparkey! Him comin'. Come to mi Sparkey.

Noise comes from the open grave.

Heather   I wan' go home.

Clarkey *jumps out of the grave.* **Heather** *screams.* **Clarkey** *chases her.* **Heather** *runs in fear but eventually stops when she recognises the person chasing her.*

Heather   Clarkey!

Clarkey   Yu turn whiter dan white Header! (*Barks like a dog, runs off.*)

Heather   Yu nasty evil lickle wretch Clarkey, I hate yu!

Heather *turns to see* **Bernice** *laughing her head off.*

Heather   Yu trick mi.

Bernice   Yu trick yerself. Why yu so stupid, Header?

Heather   I'm not stupid. I'm not!

Bernice   Yu go cry now? It was only a joke. It were Clarkey's idea.

Heather   Clarkey a dog, 'im do wat yu tell 'im.

Bernice   Don't go yet. I only wanted to give yu summin to remember us by. I go miss yu, Header.

Heather   Yu love to lie.

Bernice   I go miss yu. More dan yu realise. We is family Header.

Heather   Mi know!

Bernice   We is sisters.

Heather   Shut up.

Bernice   Yer daddy is my daddy.

Heather   I'll punch yu hard, yu nuh.

Bernice   Both our muddas were fightin' las' night, I hear dem. I hear de trut'.

Heather   Why yu love to lie?

Bernice   Yu shoulda hear my mudda scream, it wake de dead. Yer daddy sleep wid him dead brudda's wife!

Heather   No!

Bernice   It trut'.

Heather   No!

Sound of a dog growling.

Bernice   Wat were dat?

Heather   Bernice!

Bernice   It not mi.

Heather   Sparkey?

Dog barks.

Heather\Bernice   Jesus!

The girls run for their lives.

Scene Two

Present day. The same graveyard.

Heather *is alone. She is standing over a new grave. She kneels down over the flat headstone. She sweeps the dust off the headstone with her hands, then replaces the flowers with fresh ones.*

Heather   There you are, son.

Janet (*enters*)   Tell yer Mum yu don't half walk fast. Didn't yu hear me calling yer? Mum?

Heather *can hear her daughter but does not reply.* **Janet** *just stands for a moment, watching her mother, not saying anything. She finally goes over when she can hear her mother crying.*

Janet   Yu want a tissue?

Heather   No. You keep them, you need them.

Janet   I aint sneezed since we got here.

Heather   Don't tempt fate, Janet.

Janet   Mus' be the clean air.

Heather   You call this clean? Did you think the house was clean when we got there? Or was that my imagination?

Janet   No Mum.

Heather   I'm going to kill Bernice when I see her. How hard is it to meet us at the airport, how hard is that?

Janet   She sent Clarkey.

Heather   Clarkey sent himself. He's bin covering for her since school.

Janet   He's really sweet aint he?

Heather   He's not a dog, Janet.

Janet *sneezes.*

Heather   See, that is you tempting fate.

Janet   Bloody hell.

Heather   Come on.

Janet   Ware's my tissue? (*Searches for tissue and continues to sneeze.*)

Heather (*can't bear to look*)   Hurry up.

Janet   It's not my fault.

Heather   I can't bear to look at you when you are like this.

Janet   So don't look.

Heather   Why do you always sneeze?

Janet   I got allergies.

Heather   And every five minutes you have a cold. I bet you don't eat any vegetables at all, do you?

Janet   Yeah.

Heather   You are puttin' on weight.

Janet (*feeling embarrassed*)   Mum!

Heather   Go on a diet.

Janet   Diets don't work.

Heather   You don't work. You've got no discipline. I can draw up a balanced diet for you if you want.

Janet   No thanks. (*Stops sneezing. Blows her nose. Looks down at it afterwards.*)

Heather (*disgusted*)   Don't look at it! You're not pregnant again are you?

Janet   Wat yu mean again? Yu carry on like I'm dropping them every five minutes. No I'm not.

Heather   Then you are putting on weight.

Janet   Awright then I am.

Heather   You carry on like this my dear, you'll end up like those big, fat, awful women that never leave their houses.

Janet   Oh stop it.

Heather   They just sit down all day watching tele and stuffing their faces all day, the slobs.

Janet   Fine.

Heather   Look at your grandmother.

Janet   Oh leave her alone. Gran aint no slob.

Heather   I know, but see how slow she walks now. Why do you think she never came with us? You have a good look at her when you see her next, Janet. That is what happens when you reach the end . . .

Janet   Yu are so out of order.

Heather   . . . when you let yourself go. Diet! It won't kill you to try.

Janet   I'll try. (*Looks around.*) So this is it? Our family. Am I gonna end up here as well?

Heather   Ignore her, son.

Janet   Sorry broth, I'm jus' makin' bad jokes again. Peace.
(*Spots a headstone.*) Sparkey? Who's that?

Heather   Come away from there, Janet.

Janet   Cousin, uncle?

Heather   Come away from there.

Janet   Wat? Yer as white as a sheet, man.

Heather   Don't be so stupid.

Janet   Look in a mirror if yu don't believe me.

Heather   Sparkey was my dog.

Janet   Yu had a dog?

Heather   Obviously.

Janet   Yu hate dogs.

Heather   I know.

Janet   Remember when I was eight, yu wouldn't let me
have one.

Heather   Yes.

Janet   Wat 'appened to it?

Heather   It got hit by a car.

Janet   Sorry. Funeral went well.

Heather   It wasn't enough. The pastor didn't know him.
What did he know about Andrew and his life?

Janet   Yu wanted him buried here.

Heather   I didn't want him buried there.

Janet   Yu can't blame a whole country for wat happened.

Heather   How english of yu.

Janet   We're not the only ones who missed him. All his
mates wanted to say goodbye.

Heather   They had the memorial service to do that.

Janet   That was last year.

Heather   This was our service. The family.

Janet   Yeah, and wat about Dad?

Heather   What about him? If he cared, he'd be here.

Janet   He doesn't even know, Mum.

Heather   What do you want me to do, traipse through the whole of America to find him?

Janet   No.

Heather   He doesn't want to be found.

Janet   I'm jus' . . .

Heather   . . . You don't know that by now?

Janet   Awright forget it!

Heather (*clocks her daughter's face*)   Don't do that.

Janet   Don't do wat?

Heather   That look.

Janet   Wat look?

Heather   The same look your father used to pull.

Janet   I'm not Dad, awright?

Heather   So lose the look.

Janet   Jesus!

Heather   Janet why have you come here?

Janet   He was my brother, Mum.

Heather   No, why have you followed me here?

Janet (*sarcastic*)   I fancied a walk. To see if yer awright.

Heather   Well I am, so you can go back to the house and call your boyfriend now.

Janet   Ryan. Can't yu say his name just once?

Heather   Maybe if you had stayed in school . . .

Janet (*knows what is coming*)   . . . No!

Heather   . . . instead of skiving off with your worthless friends, trying to run a restaurant with your aimless boyfriend . . . getting yourself pregnant.

Janet   Oh yu had to bloody go there. (*Smug.*) Don't do that.

Heather   Don't do what?

Janet   That look.

Heather (*getting defensive*)   What look?

Janet   The disappointed look.

Heather (*getting wound up*)   Child!

Janet   Yu don't believe me, fine, I don't care.

Heather *raises her hands. She has had enough of this.*

Heather   I'll come back later, son.

Janet (*pleads with her*)   Oh Mum!

Heather *leaves.*

Janet (*to the grave*)   Summin I said? Wat about yu then, yu got summin to say? Don't talk to Mum like that, yer embarrassed to be my brother? Like I don't know? Yu aint exactly wat I had in mind for a big brother yu know? (*Laughs.*) 'Yu ever see Andrew do that?' She aint seen half the things yu've done, ennit broth? I know wat yer tryin' to do. Well yu can piss off. Yu weren't nice to me either, I'm supposed to drain my tears over yu, little mummy's boy? Move! All I have to do is tell her right, jus' open my mouth,

let her know wat her precious little boy was really like, yu
think I won't . . .

A gust of wind comes sweeping through.

Janet (*feels something*) Broth?

Scene Three

Outside **Bernice**'s.

Clarkey *is with* **Bernice**.

Clarkey   Drink it.

Bernice   No man.

Clarkey   Drink it!

Bernice   Move yerself!

Clarkey   Yu wan' stay drunk all day?

Bernice   Clarkey, I'd rather be drunk dan drink wat yu
call tea!

Clarkey   Yu turn up yer nose at mi mudda's home-made
tea?

Bernice   Clarkey, no offence right, but it nasty!

Clarkey   Fine den!

Bernice   Oh Clarkey man!

Clarkey   Yu wan' feel like shit, gwan!

Bernice   Relax man, a joke mi a mek. Smile nuh man!

Clarkey   Mi nuh feel like it.

Bernice   Wat mi do?

Clarkey   Ware de hell yu bin, Bernice?

Bernice   Lord Jesus, I go down Kingston to si Judy.

Clarkey   Yu nuh even tell mi.

Bernice   Oh we marry now?

Clarkey   Yu jus' gwan. It's mi the one who have to pick up yer sister Bernice, mi never feel so shame in all mi life.

Bernice   Oh shush.

Clarkey   Shameful!

Bernice   Shush! Deh settle in?

Clarkey   No tanks to yu.

Bernice   Yes mi hear yu now.

Clarkey   Jus' about.

Bernice   How is she?

Clarkey   She seem awright. I tell yu if it were mi, man, I dunno if I coulda speak. Yu shoulda bin here to greet her, Bernice.

Bernice   Awright nuh man! Is why yu love to chat so?

Clarkey   So wat yu do dat so important in Kingston?

Bernice   Yu nosey eeh!

Clarkey   Yu go tell mi?

Bernice   I go si Judy like mi say.

Clarkey   And?

Bernice   And wat?

Clarkey   No tell mi no fish stories right.

Bernice   Oooh, Clarkey big man now!

Clarkey   Woman!

Bernice   Awright! But yu go get mad.

Clarkey   Jus' tell mi.

Bernice   Judy have a friend, right? She live downtown an' las' week her daddy dead.

Clarkey   Huh huh?

Bernice   But him leave behind a whole heap of bills, soon deh get thrown outta de house.

Clarkey   Wat dis have to do wid yu?

Bernice   Wait nuh! But before de daddy dead right, he leave sum big insurance policy, but dem can't find it, deh search all over de house, cursing deh daddy name while deh doin' it, ca' when he was alive, he was shrewd, too shrewd fer him own good. Him love him secret hidin' places to put away him tings, no one knows ware he leave de policy.

Clarkey   So why he never tell dem ware de policy is?

Bernice   Ca' him never know he go get lick in de head by sum mule las' month and die next day. Fool! Him must tink him go die by gettin' old and sick, dat way him got time to tell him family an' wat deh have to do.

Clarkey   Is ware yu come into dis?

Bernice   Judy tell dem about mi.

Clarkey   And?

Bernice   And deh ask if I coulda contact de fudda, find out ware him hide de policy.

Clarkey   I knew it!

Bernice   Eighty dollars deh give mi Clarkey.

Clarkey   Yu never learn.

Bernice   Oh shut up.

Clarkey   So yu talk to him?

Bernice   Yeah man, mi hear 'im.

Clarkey *shakes his head.*

Bernice   Mi hear 'im, man!

Clarkey   So ware 'im hide de policy?

Bernice   'Im nuh tell mi, and before yu gimme any of yer stupid look right, 'im say he not go tell ca' 'im accuse 'im 'ole family a' bin gravedigger, deh nuh care 'bout him when 'im alive, so why 'im should care now 'im dead?

Clarkey   I jus' hope yu give dem back deh money.

Bernice   Yu such a boy scout, yu nuh.

Clarkey   I'd rather be dat dan sum wort'less tief.

Bernice   I don't tief, I provide a service. Bernice Stuart, spiritualist advisor.

Clarkey   I bet deh catch yu out ennit? Deh find out and chase yu outta Kingston?

Bernice   No.

Clarkey   Deh nuh hurt yu, right?

Bernice   Nuttin 'appened. Mi fine.

Clarkey   Downtown a rough place, Bernice.

Bernice   I got de gift, Clarkey.

Clarkey *shakes his head.*

Bernice   Oh yu mek mi so mad.

Clarkey   Mi mek yu drunk too? Yu tink yu go find wat yu wan' at de bottom of de bottle?

Bernice   Yu not mi mudda.

Clarkey   Nor are yu.

Bernice   Awright! Yu jus' shut yer mout'. Yu cross the line now.

Clarkey   An' yu too old to farm de fool.

Bernice   Oh cha rass man.

Clarkey   It nuh right.

Bernice   Yu go tell mi wat is?

Clarkey   Yu know.

Bernice   Marry yu. Be a mudda to yer wort'less son, lookin' after yer sick mudda. Clarkey mi dunno if I ready fer all dat.

Clarkey   Woman yu is forty-seven now, forty-seven. If yu don't know, is when?

Bernice   Wat yu si in mi Clarkey? Why yu want fer marry mi? Yu better off wid Junie Riley, she aways like yu.

Clarkey   Junie Riley only have one eye, an' she can't si nuh better wid dat one.

Bernice   Remember when she walk right in Miss Devereaux's shop? (*Laughs.*) Straight through de window she go, like sum fool.

Clarkey   Woman can't even look after she self let alone my mudda.

Bernice   Si, deh yu go, yu want nursemaid.

Clarkey   If yu coulda let mi finish, yu never let mi finish.

Bernice   Sorry.

Clarkey   It's not she mi love.

Bernice   Yu is a good man Clarkey . . .

Clarkey   . . . Don't say dat.

Bernice   And yu gwan 'bout not lettin' yu finish.

Clarkey   Sorry.

Bernice   I need more time, man.

Clarkey   How much more time yu need?

Enter **Janet** *with bags of shopping.*

Clarkey (*points to Bernice*)   Well look who mi find.

Janet   Hello Auntie.

Bernice   Lickle Janet is dat yu? Girl yu get round, yu nuh.

Janet   Yu awright?

Bernice   Mi fine darling, fine! Look at yu now. Is why yu stand so far? Mi nuh bite, much. Come. (*Gives her a hug.*) Lickle Janet! Awright den, so ware mi beautiful lickle great niece, Tamia right? Ware she den?

Janet   Back home wid her dad.

Bernice   Oh yu shoulda bring her, child. Mi can't wait to see her. It so good to have yu all here. Sorry mi not here to greet yu, and de state of de house, an' there were no food, yer auntie had tings to do, yu nuh. She a busy woman, yu know how it is.

Janet   Don't worry about it.

Clarkey   Don't go feelin' sorry fer her, Janet. Mek her feel bad, it wat she deserve.

Bernice   Yes tank yu, Clarkey.

Clarkey   Who want sum tea?

Bernice   Say no.

Clarkey   Mi hear dat. (*Goes inside.*)

Bernice   Janet look at yu! How long it bin?

Janet   I dunno, ages. I was still at school.

Bernice   Look 'pon yu! Yu is a woman now. Mudda. Yu still have man? Wat him name?

Janet   Ryan.

Bernice   Oooh Ryan! 'Im fit? (*Roars.*) It's awright, long as yu hang on to him tail dough, before sum oder gal come drag 'im away, like mi. Smile Janet, mi mek joke.

Janet   I know.

Bernice (*acting really offended*)   Wat yu mean yu know? Yu don't tink I can get man? Listen right, yer auntie have more dan she fair share of fit young man, and I mean fit! Right? (*Bursts out laughing.*) Child listen right, if yu want spend time wid mi, yu have to loosen up, yu hear? Nuh come like yer mudda, mi beg yu.

Janet *does not quite get* **Bernice***'s sense of humour.* **Bernice** *laughs again.*

Bernice   Lord, yu english fer trut'. (*Turns serious.*) Look, listen right, I so sorry about Andy.

Janet   Thanks Auntie.

Bernice   He was a lovely bwai Janet. Brock my heart when I hear de news, brock my heart.

Janet   Yeah.

Heather *enters.*

Bernice   MADAME!

Heather   Shown yourself at last then have you?

Bernice   How yu doin' sister?

Heather   I'm doing fine, Bernice.

Bernice   Yu have no big sisterly hug fer mi?

Heather   Don't be ridiculous.

Bernice   Come let mi hold yu.

Heather   You stay where you are.

Bernice   Come nuh! (*Grabs her, lifts her up.*)

Heather (*protests*)   Bernice!

Bernice   Gal yu get heavy!

Heather   So put me down.

Bernice *obeys.*

Heather   Now let me go.

Bernice   No.

Heather   What do you mean no?

Bernice   Yu nuh say de magic word.

Heather   Will you *please* let me go.

Bernice (*thinks about it for a second*)   No.

Heather   I said the magic word.

Bernice   Mi happy to si yu!

Heather (*pleads*)   Bernice!

Bernice (*releases her*)   Oh yes, mi ferget yu turn english now.

Heather   Where the hell have you been?

Bernice   I jus' love de way yu talk now, yu si.

Heather (*putting on the accent*)   Is ware yu bin?

Bernice   Around.

Heather   Where?

Bernice   Jus' around.

Janet (*feeling awkward*)   Right then, I'll leave yu two to it, yeah?

Heather   Where are you going?

Janet   Jus' inside, gonna help Clarkey. (*Exits.*)

Bernice   Alone at last, hey?

Heather   Stop it.

Bernice   Come on Header, one more hug?

Heather   Why won't you answer my question?

Bernice   Ca' mi nuh like de question.

Heather   You should have been here.

Bernice   Yu know mi awready Header, can't keep still fer anyting.

Heather   I also know you can't hold a broom in your hand. I can't believe the state you left the house in.

Bernice   It's my house.

Heather   Daddy left it to me, Bernice.

Bernice   And yu love to throw dat in mi face.

Heather   So I don't have a right to speak? I'm supposed to walk around all that mess, and pretend it's not there? Is that right, is that what you are saying? Are you listening to me? (*Sees* **Bernice** *looking at her watch.*) What are you doing?

Bernice   Two minute. We nuh si each oder fer years an' years an it tek two minute fer us to fight.

Heather   Fine, make your jokes.

Bernice   Gimme a chance to say sorry?

Heather   Go on then.

Bernice   I sorry I miss de funeral.

Heather   Did you find something better to do?

Bernice   Fine, I deserve dat.

Heather   That doesn't even come close.

Bernice   Well if yu feel like dat why don't yu jus' go home? Yu done wat yu wan', yu buried yer son, go home.

Heather   You should have been here, that's all I'm saying to you.

Bernice   Why? Yu carry on like yu wan' fer mi to tek care a yu?

Heather   I do not need anyone taking care of me!

Bernice   So wat yu chat 'bout?

Heather   Nothing.

Bernice (*trying to lighten the situation*)   Slip yu?

Heather   Just buy a broom Bernice, one broom.

Bernice   Yu want fer mi to go right now?

Heather   Outside doesn't look much better. Don't you think it's time you painted it again?

Bernice   Nope.

Heather   It's a disgrace.

Bernice   Daddy painted it.

Heather (*surprised*)   Daddy?

Bernice   Is why yu look surprise?

Heather   I didn't know that.

Bernice   Now yu do.

Heather   Back home Mum had to drag Daddy off his couch, beg him to do any work around the house.

Bernice   Well 'im weren't in England when he paint de house.

Heather   I am not here to fight, OK?

Bernice   Den don't talk.

Heather   I'm going inside.

Bernice   Yu carry on like yu dead too.

Heather   I'm tired.

Bernice   Watever yu say, sister.

Scene Four

Graveyard.

Janet *is alone.*

Janet (*laughing*) . . . then she lifted her up, right in the air –
yu shoulda seen it man, Mum's face. Strong man. 'Member
when she told us once, she could pick up a whole horse by
herself? And yu believed her, yer soft git. And yu were
afraid of her, cos she loved tellin' ghost stories, hidin' under
my covers whenever we heard the footsteps. 'Auntie Bernice
is comin' to get me!' That was yu. Scared little Andy, I
remember that, yu fool. Yu know summin, it's weird, right,
but I feel like . . . Andy, yu watchin' me? Andy? Shut the
fuck up Janet. Hear wat, Mum knows 'bout the caff so yu
know wass gonna 'appen now? She gonna go on and on
about it, yu know how she stay, me and Ryan should sell up,
prove her right, Janet's fucked up again. Cos compared to
yu, I'm nuttin, ennit broth? I hate, fuckin' hate yu. I hate
yu. I don't miss yu, wid yer snidy little bitchy comments,
who yu tryin' to impress? Then yu actin' all hard, givin' it
large, wat were yu thinkin' man? Wat was goin' thru yer
head? Now yu tryin' to mek me feel bad, wat yu want?

*She starts stamping on the headstone, she kicks the flowers, picks up
some pebbles and dirt and throws them at it.*

Janet (*in a rage*)   Wat . . .

*She feels the wind again. She turns around suddenly. Someone is there
with her, she can feel it. She can hear something.*

Janet (*terrified*) No.

Scene Five

Outside **Bernice**'s *house.*

Heather *is with* **Clarkey**.

Heather (*laughing*)   No!

Clarkey   It trut'.

Heather   Stop it.

Clarkey   No, listen. Yu remember Teddy Jeffries and h̄im brudda, right? They never get on, right? Yu remember? Argue, Jesus, like cat an' dog.

Heather   I remember them.

Clarkey   So when him brudda dead, Teddy carry like he got no care in de world. Tellin' him wife he go do wat him want, drink and gamble whenever him feel. She say 'Nossir,' him say 'Shut yer mout' woman.' So, him wife decide she go teach him a lesson. She go si Bernice, give her fifty dollars to tell Teddy she si a vision of him brudda, telling him he must give up him bad ways, oderwise him go come back as a black fowl and follow him everywhere till him drop down dead. So Teddy wife get deh bwoy Jody to buy de blackest fowl him si, follow him daddy, no get catch, and mek sure de fowl near him daddy. Den, pass de word all over town, that everybody mus' pretend deh can't si de fowl, it's Teddy's mind ca' him drinkin' too much dat mek him and nobody else si de fowl. It go on fer a whole week, Teddy losin' him mind. 'Wa gwan, wa gwan, lord help mi nuh, mi lose mi mind!'

Heather   So wat did he do?

Clarkey   'Im shoot de fowl! 'Im get him daddy old shotgun an' blast de ting into de next life. Right in the middle a' de street. Him scream, 'Yu all si dat?' Dem si it awright, policeman as well, dem haul 'im arse right into jail. When him find out de trut', Teddy go after him wife, go after him bwoy.

Heather   Bernice?

Clarkey   She hide out in mi yard. It tek a whole month fer Teddy to calm down. I tell yu, Header, dat sister a' yours.

Heather   She want tekin' in hand.

Clarkey   Yu talk like I don't know dat.

Heather   Hurry up man, make a honest woman of her.

Clarkey   It she mi waitin' on. Maybe I should mek joke, and say mi want fer marry yu.

Heather   Yer mad if yu want do that. She'll come round Clarkey.

Clarkey   When mi dead?

Heather   She'll see you.

Clarkey   Si wat?

Heather   That you're a good man.

Clarkey (*cringes*)   Why yu women love to say dat?

Heather   But it's true. You arranged everything for me.

Clarkey   Who else go do it?

Heather   And yu still know how to make me laugh. Only yu, man.

Clarkey   Wat, no one mek yu laugh in Englan'?

Heather *shakes her head.*

Clarkey   Yu nuh laugh at all?

Heather   Not for a while.

Clarkey   I still can't believe it.

Heather   You telling me that?

Clarkey   Him only a lickle bwoy when mi las' si him.

Heather   That's how I try to see him sometimes, as a little boy. Riding on his bike when he was what, eleven. Wearing his Arsenal kit. Do you love your son, Clarkey?

Clarkey   Wort'less wretch!

Heather   But you do love him?

Clarkey   Yeah, so?

Heather   When was the last time you told him that?

Clarkey   (*getting embarrassed*)   Header?

Heather   What?

Clarkey   Come on.

Heather   Is that such a hard question?

Clarkey   Mi can't remember.

Heather   You'll be surprised how many parents say the same thing. They know they love their children, they feel it every day, but they don't say it. Where I live right, I see so many parents, yellin' at their kids, to do this an' that, fighting with them, throwing them out, swearing. You wouldn't believe it man, they haven't got a clue. They don't deserve to have children. It never occurs to them for one minute in their stupid minds, that might be the last thing they ever say to them. Because an hour from now they might get knocked down by a bus, get hurt in a car crash, or get stabbed . . .

Clarkey   Header . . .

Heather   And when that happens? They try to remember all the good things they did with their children, the nice things they said, but the only thing that keeps coming back is the last thing they said to them, the last time they saw them. So angry, full of hate, just for a moment, a split bloody second, but it keeps coming back.

Clarkey   So wat yu want dem parents to do? Tell dem pikne every blasted day deh love dem?

Heather   Why not?

Clarkey   Ca' if I tell Neil I love 'im every day right, all him go do is laugh, an' all I go do is knock off 'm head!

Children are good, Header, but deh also renk! Dass it. Yu
can't beat yerself up.

Heather   He wanted to join a band, Clarkey, he wanted
to quit college in his final year, and go join a stupid band, I
had to say something . . .

Clarkey   Yes.

Heather   I couldn't just sit there and nod my head.

Clarkey   No.

Heather   I didn't raise him to be like his father. He was
walking through some seedy little street, thass where
Nicholls saw him, where that animal kill him.

Clarkey   No, no, don't.

Heather   He took him from me.

Clarkey   Mi know.

Heather   He got away with it.

Clarkey   Yes.

Heather   And they all jus' stood by and let him do it.

Clarkey   He's a bastard, Header, he's a sunafabitch.

Heather   They're all bastards, Clarkey, they're all sons of
bitches. Thirty-two years of my life man, thirty-two years,
paying into their system. All I wanted back was justice, not
lies, just justice. Andrew never started trouble in his whole
life.

Clarkey   Course he didn't.

Heather   I raised him better than that.

Clarkey   Course yu do.

Heather   He was a good boy.

Clarkey   Wat yu go do, Header?

Heather   I don't know. As soon as I heard the verdict, all I wanted was to get out of there, get my boy out of there. He was too good for that country anyway.

Clarkey   Is why yu nuh stay? Dis yer home gal.

Heather   Don't let Bernice hear yu say that.

Clarkey   Is who yer daddy leave 'im house to? Dis ware yu belong.

Heather   I could go back.

Clarkey   Go back fer wat?

Heather   Get justice for Andrew. I don't want to feel like I let him down.

Clarkey   Shut up, yu nuh let nobody down, right? Yu did yer best.

Heather   That's what my mum says. 'I did my best fer yu, Header.'

Clarkey   Come on.

Heather   I don't know wat I'm doing man, I don't know wat to feel.

Clarkey   Yu stay which part yu deh. Yu soon see how yu feel, promise yu. Den we go tek all yer problems yu see, roll dem all up in a ball, kick it right up in de sky, let it go, straight past through de cloud dem. Past de sun, pass de moon, outer space! Yu hearin' mi?

Heather *smiles.*

Clarkey   Wat?

Heather   Bernice is such an idiot.

Clarkey   Gwan tell her, mi nuh stop yu.

Heather   Tell me another story, Clarkey. Come on man, make me laugh again.

Bernice *enters, singing. She sees* **Heather** *and* **Clarkey**.

Bernice   Well look 'pon dis! My two favourite people in de whole world, chatting. How nicey, eeh? Nice.

Clarkey   Yu drunk again?

Bernice   Sorry mudda.

Clarkey   I mek sum drink.

Bernice   I don' want nona yer mama's blasted tea, right!

Heather   Bernice!

Bernice   Yu nuh taste it, Header, come like summin outta my behind. Yu wan' drink it? Gwan Clarkey, mek sum fer Heather, gwan.

Clarkey   Should be ashamed.

Bernice   Oh leave mi man. Hey Header, Header, who dis? (*Barks like a dog.*)

Heather   Stop it.

Bernice   Ca' yu know who it is.

Clarkey   Enuff Bernice.

Bernice   Two a' yu carry on like yu old people. (*Mimics.*) Sparkey, Sparkey, yu supposed to be dead, Sparkey.

Heather   No one's laughing.

Bernice   But yu remember don't yu, wat we did. Ca' yu si Clarkey tink I am a fool, a fraud, wasting mi time, on foolishness, but yu were there sister, yu saw wat I did. Tell him.

Heather   I did. Yu did. We told everyone, but no one believed us. Jesus Christ, what is the matter with yu? Clarkey, deal wid her please.

Clarkey   Inside Bernice.

Bernice   I'm not drinkin' yer tea!

Clarkey   Yu hear mi ask yu to?

Bernice   Let go a' me.

Clarkey   Wat de hell mi do now?

Bernice   Is wat yu say to Miss Sandford?

Clarkey   I nuh say nuttin to her.

Bernice   So why she come up to mi in the street, to mi face, say how she glad she get her money back, da mi should not promise wat mi can't deliver. Wat yu do?

Clarkey   Mi pay off one a' yer debts , and dis de tanks I get.

Bernice   Is who tell yu to run my life?

Clarkey   Yu call dis a life?

Bernice   It mine.

Clarkey   Header, listen to wat yer fool of a sister go do.

Bernice   I no fool.

Clarkey   Miss Sandford lose her daughter two year ago, right? Den las' month, Bernice go budda de woman, day and night, tell how she say she get message from the daughter on de oder side.

Bernice   It happened.

Clarkey   Yer fart!

Bernice   Jus' ca' yu nuh si it, it don't mean it never 'appened.

Clarkey   So she tek her money, den she tell de woman, she lose her daughter.

Bernice   Dat 'appens as well.

Clarkey   And she spend all she money.

Bernice   De daughter come back, Clarkey.

Clarkey (*laughs*)   When?

Bernice   Yu tink Miss Sandford go believe mi now?

Clarkey   No one do.

Bernice *throws her bottle at him.*

Heather   Stop it.

Bernice   Gwan, laugh 'bout dat now. Gwan! Yu still love mi now Clarkey?

Clarkey   Yu want fer mi to say no, don't it? Yu want end dis, yu tell mi to my face. I si yu Header. (*Exits.*)

Heather   You always love to hurt that man. One day he won't come back.

Bernice   Clarkey a ball, yu throw 'im against a wall, 'im aways come back.

Heather   Don't be so sure.

Bernice   Still like him, right?

Heather   No.

Bernice   Yu used to.

Heather   When I was twelve.

Bernice   Marry him if yu want.

Heather   Go to bed.

Bernice   Yu look after him mudda. De old bitch.

Heather   Look Berni . . . Mother? Are you telling me that woman is still alive?

Bernice   He nuh mention her?

Heather   No. I jus' assumed she was dead. Bloody hell, Mrs Clark! How old is she now?

Bernice   I don't blasted know. A hundred or summin.

Heather   Even when we were little girls, she was still an old woman.

Bernice   She jus' won't die de old cow! And she miserable, Jesus! 'When yu go marry mi bwoy, yu farm de fool too much Bernice Stuart. Come like yer mudda. Is why yu nuh drink mi tea?' I'm sure she stayin' alive jus' to spite mi, yu nuh. Everytime I'm round deh, I love to slam all de doors real hard. I hope it give her a shock, mek she fall down dead from her heart, but nuh, she still deh.

Heather   It's not his fault he has a mother like that.

Bernice   Mi know.

Heather   So what are you waiting for? Marry him.

Bernice   Header, do yu really tink I would ever let any old bitch like she come between mi and a man I love from de bottom of my heart?

Heather   You have got to tell him.

Bernice   How can I wid him puppy eyes?

Heather   He's not a dog. Tell him the truth if that's how you really feel . . .

Bernice   Oh so it yu dat turn into my mudda now.

Heather   Fine, you carry on, talk to your ghosts for the rest of your life.

Bernice   Well, we can't all be doctor.

Heather   You could have been anything you want. Clarkey was only trying to help you.

Bernice   Oh yu go mek mi cry.

Heather   He loves you, Bernice. God knows why. I've never seen a man so desperate to live with somebody.

Bernice   Dat'll suit yu won't it? Mi wid Clarkey so yu can have de house to yerself, right?

Heather   I am not interested in the bloody house.

Bernice   Why 'im leave de house to yu? Yu five thousand miles away, an' 'im give it to yu.

Heather   Don't blame me because you wasted half yer life looking after him.

Bernice   Clive Stuart loved me.

Heather   Clive Stuart loved Clive Stuart.

Bernice   Yu were jealous!

Heather   Jealous a' wat! You're just another one of his kids he's got scattered all over the planet. 'Bout mi jealous. He was a loser. Go buy yourself another bottle.

Bernice   Look 'pon she, 'im favourite daughter, when yu come back here fer 'im funeral, lording it up all up, flashing she money, Doctor Heather Mackenzie act like she better dan we. No lightning go strike her, she lucky. Different story now aint it? (*Realises what she's said.*) Mi nuh mean dat.

Heather   You did.

Bernice   It de drink dat talk.

Heather   It's yer voice mi hear.

Janet *enters, looking absolutely terrified.*

Heather   Janet? Janet wat is wrong with you?

Janet   Andy . . . Andy . . .

Heather   What . . . what are you talking about?

Janet *struggles to get the words out.*

Heather   Janet!

Janet   Andy.

Heather   What about him?

Janet *sneezes.*

Heather   Oh God.

Bernice   Janet, wat is wrong child, yu look like yu si a ghost. (*Clocks* **Janet***'s expression.*) Janet?

Janet *laughs out loud.*

Heather   You are going insane young lady.

Bernice   Can't yu si she upset about summin . . .

Heather   . . . She's makin' a fool of herself. Janet, go inside before you sneeze yerself to death.

Janet *lets out a scream in anger.*

Heather   Look at you!

Janet *screams again, right in front of her mother's face.* **Heather** *replies with a slap across the head.*

Bernice   Header!

Janet *runs inside.*

Bernice   Wa' wrong wid yu? Summin was troubling her.

Heather   Summin is aways troubling her. She got troubles coming out of her arse.

Bernice   Yu couldn't find out wat was wrong? Yu had to slap her down like dat?

Heather   Yu don't know, Bernice.

Bernice   Know wat, Header?

Heather   Yer right yer nuh, all this, completely different story.

Bernice   I didn't mean dat. Header?

Heather   Bring him to me.

Bernice   Wat?

Heather   Yu done it before. With Sparkey. Bring my boy back to me, Bernice.

Bernice   So it's now yu believe mi?

Heather   Look at her, thirty-two years of my life. Thass all I have to show for. I want my son back. Please.

Scene Six

Outside **Bernice**'s *house.* **Clarkey** *is with* **Bernice**.

Clarkey   ARE YU OUTTA YER BLASTED MIND?

Bernice   Mi knew mi shouldn't have tell yu.

Clarkey   I never hear anyting more stupid in my entire life.

Bernice   Clarkey I can do dis.

Clarkey   Is dis yer way a mekin' yer daddy love yu?

Bernice   She need mi Clarkey, fer de first time in her life, she need mi. I sick an' tired a' everybody pushin' mi aside, all mi life, well no more.

Clarkey   Yu ever si mi do dat to yu?

Bernice   Yu never believed in wat I can do, not fer a second.

Clarkey   Yu comin' home wid mi right now yu understand? Stop farmin de arse wid yerself woman!

Bernice *laughs.*

Clarkey   Stop dat, yu love to mek fun a' mi.

Bernice   Is ware yu learn to act so big?

Clarkey   Mama aways said yu want tekin' in hand . . .

Bernice   Yer mudda talk shit. Yu wan' leave her, and dat so-called son a' yours.

Clarkey   Deh my family.

Bernice   I know. So go home. Clarkey go home man.

Clarkey   No! I wan' si yu do dis. I want si yu standing in de middle a dat grave and talk to dat bwoy, mi wan' si yu talk. Yu say I never believe yu, prove mi wrong den. Come!

Bernice   How de hell yu expect mi to do anyting wid yu standin' deh?

Clarkey   Nuh mek excuse.

Bernice   I nuh mek excuse. My mind need to be clear, of all thoughts, except dem of de spirits.

Clarkey   A' course.

Bernice   Yu si? Dat exactly wat mi talking about. How de hell can I manage to do anyting, wid yu aways deh.

Clarkey   Yu blamin' mi?

Bernice   Yer aways in my way.

Clarkey   But yu can't do it.

Bernice   Clarkey yu have to stop dis awright. Yu know yu do. Mi nuh love yu.

Clarkey   Shut up.

Bernice   It trut'.

Clarkey   Yu mad?

Bernice   Clarkey?

Clarkey   Yu wan' lie down, yu nuh feel well.

Bernice   I tellin' yu, to yer face! I bin feelin' like dis fer years man, but yu too stupid to listen.

Clarkey   Is why yu say dis fer?

Bernice   Yu an' mi more like brudda an' sister, it nuh right, it nuh feel right.

Clarkey   It feel right to mi. Why yu want dash 'way wat we have?

Bernice   Ca' it trut', hear mi please!

Clarkey   So wat mi do now?

Bernice   Marry Junie Riley, mi nuh know.

Clarkey   Yu nuh care.

Bernice   Right!

Clarkey   Truth finally leave yer mout'.

Bernice   Mi never want fer hurt yu Clarkey.

Clarkey (*snaps*)   No budda wid dat!

Bernice   I try . . .

Clarkey   Yu nuh try, yu gwan on about love, yu can't even si love when it right under yer nose. Yu carry on wid yer spirit dem.

Bernice   Tek care a' yerself Clarkey.

Clarkey   Yu wan' follow yer own advice.

Scene Seven

Graveside.

Janet *is alone with her brother.*

Janet (*laughing*)   No! No it was yu! Don't lie Andy. I distracted Mum, yu were the one who unscrewed the top of the salt bottle, and I dared yu to, cos it was my turn to dare yu remember? Shame! The look on her face, remember that? I thought she was gonna croak man. The salt went all over her chips. And as usual she looked at me like I was the one who did it. Like butter wouldn't melt in yer mouth. You were her favourite, you know yu were. Who she give the belt to? Thank yu. (*Mocks.*) Yu got licks, yu got shit. I'm jus' stating a fact thass all. (*Aside.*) Virgin! Sorry. (*Aside.*) Short arse. Yer dead and yu still can't take a joke. Andy hold up, hold up man. I wanna ask yu summin? Can I, yu know, touch yu?

Janet *reaches out for her brother's hand.*

Janet   Am I doing it, am I touchin' yer? Oh man this is weird. Yu know yu really scared me the oder day yu bastard. Yu tryin' to kill me or wat, yu want me lined up next to yu or summin? Why me? Why not Mum? She loves yu, she doesn't love me. (*She listens.*) I can't tell her that. I can't tell her that. It was your fault. Kiss my arse, I aint doin' it. Wat chance? Wat bloody chance could I have wid her?

Heather *and* **Bernice** *enter.*

Heather   This has to work.

Bernice   It'll work.

Janet   Will wat work?

Heather   What are you doing here?

Janet   Nuttin special. Wat yu doin'?

Heather   Nothing.

Janet   Come on.

Heather   It does not concern you. Come let's go Bernice.

Bernice *walks around the field.*

Heather   Bernice?

Janet   What's goin' on here Mum?

Heather   Shush! Bernice?

Bernice *senses something.*

Heather   What, what is it?

Bernice   Deh's sum troubled spirits here man.

Heather   Andrew?

Janet   Andy?

Heather   Where is he? Let me talk to him.

Bernice   Hold on, mi never say it were Andy.

Heather   Who den?

Bernice   Jus' spirits. Dem don' run up an' tell mi who deh are yu nuh, it tek time first. Deh wan' fer know if I can be trusted.

Heather   Well hurry up and say yes.

Bernice   Ease up nuh!

Janet   Yu trying to speak to Andy?

Bernice   Maybe, why?

Janet   Nuttin.

Bernice *walks around the graveyard with eyes closed tight.*
Heather *follows her.*

Heather   Bernice? Andrew? Andrew, yu there boy?

Bernice   Quiet!

Heather   It's yer mother.

Bernice   Yu want mi to do dis or not?

Heather   Of course I do.

Bernice   Den shut up. Yu'll scare dem.

Heather   Jus' get him.

Bernice   I'm tryin'. Andrew? Andrew? Yu deh bwoy? (*Pretends she can sense something.*)

Heather   Wat is it?

Bernice   Shush.

Janet   Wat she say?

Heather   Shush!

Janet   I only asked.

Heather   Janet! Sorry Bernice.

Bernice   Someone's here. I can feel dem.

Janet   Who?

Bernice   Andrew! Is dat yu bwoy?

Heather   I want to talk to him.

Bernice   Ware yu bin?

Heather   Let me speak to him.

Bernice   Yer mama here Andrew, she want talk to yu, yu ready?

Heather   Where is he?

Bernice   'Im right here, right here in front a' yu.

Janet   Wat?

Heather   Oh God! Andrew? How you doing son?

Janet   Mum?

Bernice   He misses you.

Heather   Oh darling I miss you too.

Bernice   'Im standing right beside yu now.

Janet   Mum!

Bernice   'Im get so big! 'Im right there, Header.

Heather *closes her eyes and imagines she can feel touching her son's face.*

Janet   Mum listen to me.

Heather   Move!

Janet   Listen.

Bernice (*grabs* **Janet***'s arm*)   Wat yu think yer doing?

Janet   Wat do yu think yer doing?

Bernice   She get her son back.

Janet   Oh really? Yu are sick!

Bernice   Watch yer mout' gal.

Janet   Don't threaten me.

Heather   My boy.

Janet (*slaps* **Heather***'s hands down*)   Yer boy isn't there, Mum.

Heather   What yu doing?

Janet   All yer touching is air!

Heather   Look if you don't believe that is up to you.

Janet   But I do.

Bernice   Go away child.

Heather   Right now.

Janet   Andy is here, Mum, but he's talking to me not her.

Bernice   Yu have de gift?

Heather   Janet! Don't do this to me.

Janet   Doin' wat? I aint hurtin' yu, I've never meant to hurt yu.

Heather   Andrew, yu still here? Yu still here boy?

Janet   'You are going back to college, young man. I don't know what you have to do to grow some sense back into your head, but you had better do it, and you'd better do it now!'

Heather (*stunned*)   Wat?

Janet   It was the last thing you said to him weren't it? He just told me to say it Mum. (*Relaying.*) Your pager went off, some emergency at the hospital. Andy swore at you, then he stormed out of the house. He just told me, he's telling me. Thass wat happened the last time you saw him alive.

Heather   He told you before he died.

Janet   Mum, I'm not lying.

Heather (*confused*)   What the hell is going on here?

Bernice   Header come on!

Janet   She's lying, I'm telling the truth, I swear to yu. Get her to ask Andy summin, summin only yu two would know. Do it, Mum. Trust me for once in yer life, ask her right now! I know yu've aways hated me, Mum, I've felt it all my life, so wat am I doin here? I got no reason to help yu, will yu ask her!

Heather   Bernice?

Bernice   Yu come to mi right, yu come and yu beg.

Heather   Ask him . . .

Bernice (*cuts her off*)   No!

Heather   You ask him where he spent his fifteenth birthday.

Bernice   Yu tink him go remember that?

Heather   He'll remember.

Bernice   Woman come to mi right, on her hands and knees . . .

Heather   Are you going to ask him or not?

Bernice   'Bring my boy back to mi Bernice!'

Heather   You can't do it. He spent the night in hospital, he had food poisoning, I stayed up all night with him, he was so scared. I could kill you.

Bernice (*laughs*)   Woman love to moan eeh? I give her wat she want.

Heather   I wanted my son.

Bernice   I gave yu wat yu needed, to believe.

Heather   I'm selling the house. You hear me Bernice, I'm going to throw you out on the bloody street. One thing I ask you to do for me!

Bernice   So why yu ask mi fer? Yu so good, yu so perfect, yu nuh mek mistake.

Heather   Yu really want to hurt me.

Bernice   Yu hurt yerself. Least Daddy have de strength to know 'im mek a mistake.

Heather   Don't compare me to him.

Bernice   So wat yu doin' here, Header? Wat yu need mi fer?

Heather   I didn't fail my son, right? And I want him to tell me that, Bernice, I need him to tell me.

Janet   Yu didn't fail him, Mum. But he was thinking of quitting college though.

Heather   No!

Janet   He jus' told me.

Heather   No! He was winding me up, Janet, you know what he was like. Isn't that true, son? Tell her.

Janet   No Mum . . .

Heather   You think I don't know my son, Janet? My child? You think I didn't know about those stupid games he played just to get attention? You were just teasing me, Andrew, you were joking. Come on boy! Talk to me.

Janet   He didn't want to fight yu.

Heather   I don't want to hear another word. Why would Andrew contact you?

Janet   I don't know.

Heather   Yu were always jealous of him.

Janet   Oh it really sticks in your throat don't it? That he's talking to me not yu, yer precious little boy.

Heather   You're just like your father Janet, you're weak.

Janet   Fuck yu both! (*Exits.*)

Bernice (*laughs to herself*)   Oh yes, Header no mek mistake.

Heather (*pleads*)   Andrew!

Bernice   Yu know when yu first go to England, dat night I pray fer yer plane to crash, yu nuh, right slam into de ocean. An' when yu get deh, I pray dat yu fall down sick, or get lick down by a car. I pray fer anyting that could 'appen to yu. Cos maybe den right, my daddy would remember 'im have anudda daughter.

Heather *laughs.*

Bernice   Yu tink I mek joke?

Heather   He weren't the same daddy. Soon after we step off the plane, we're walking through the terminal, I'm holding Mama's hand, she look so good, so thin, she was beautiful. Then we see this rough-looking man walking towards us, I ask 'Who is dat?' Mama say 'Das yer daddy.' 'Nuh' I say, 'dat not mi daddy, ware 'im gold tooth, ware 'im smile. Mi nuh want dat. Mi want mi daddy.'

Bernice   I wanted yu dead.

Heather   I wanted to die.

Scene Eight

Outside **Bernice***'s house. The distraught* **Janet** *is talking with* Andy.

Janet   FUCK HER. FUCK HER, FUCK HER, FUCK HER. I do mean it. Don't tell me how I feel, I hate her, listen to me, hear the words comin' outta my mouth, I hate her. No, I don't know wat yer chattin' about, leave me, I told yu before, no. Yu've never helped me in yer life, why yu stressin' me? I can't man.

Scene Nine

The graveyard.

Bernice *is alone and drunk.*

Bernice   Daddy! Oh Daddy! Yu hear mi Daddy ware yu deh? Are yu here? Or, are yu over deh! Nuh, man, yu over here, yes, yer standin' right beside mi, yes. (*Holds out her hand.*) Yu holdin' mi hand, yer daughter's hand? Yu kissin' yer lovely daughter's hand, Daddy? Daddy? Yer lovely daughter, Daddy, de one who tek care a' yu? Is Mama wid yu? Yu tell her I doin' fine right, Bernice is doin' fine! Mi had a whole heap of spirits come visit mi, yessir. Ca' dem got unfinished business in this world like Mama used to say, ca' dem loved ones want chat to dem. I is providing a service, Bernice Stuart, spiritualist advisor. Yu like de sound a' dat Daddy? No, course yu don't. Yu don't. A whole heap of spirits want talk to mi Daddy, but not yu, nossir! But yu go have to help mi now Daddy, ca' dem spirits gone, long time deh nuh talk. And I wan' fer dem to talk, oderwise mi got no life. Yu want fer dat to happen. Help mi, gwan shake up dem spirits, Daddy, tell dem to get deh backsides down here, tell dem mi not so bad, mi can help dem. Or better yet, yu come down, come talk to mi, yer daughter. Daddy? I bet if mi name was Header, yu'd come down, yu'd rush down. Not even God could stop yu. If yu love her so much, is why yu come back, is why yu leff her in England, why yu nuh stay deh? Is why yu never tell mi de one thing I wanted to hear all mi life.

Janet (*enters*)   Go away!

Bernice   Janet?

Janet   Piss off!

Bernice   Is who dat budda yu?

Janet   This fool, he won't go leave me, I got nuttin more to say to yu right!

Bernice   Si dem spirits want talk to yu now, Janet.

Janet   It's only one.

Bernice   Don't worry. Soon dem all come.

Janet   I don't want them to.

Bernice (*laughs at the irony*)   Yu don't want them to? (*Yells.*) SHE DON'T WANT DEM TO!

Janet   Help me, Auntie.

Bernice   Child I can't.

Janet   Please jus' get rid of him for me.

Bernice   I CAN'T! But yu can help mi, right? Yeah, yeah yu help mi. Speak to yer granddaddy fer mi, yu tell 'im right, yu tell 'im dat he aint nuttin but an old bastard right, and him foot stink! Deh stink! Tell him all de time I had to tek off dem man's shoes so I can put him to bed I hold mi nose in case it fall off, ca' him foot stink, right? Real bad. Yu tell him, Janet, yu go tell him.

Janet   I don't want it. Yu have it.

Bernice   If yer brudda still here right, den it ca' 'im still have business to do, an 'im walking round till it get done.

Janet (*to Andy*)   I hate yu!

Bernice   Dat nuh go mek 'im go. Yu have to mek tings right. Mi can't help yu.

Heather *enters.*

Bernice (*sees* **Heather**)   Lord I can't even get drunk in peace! (*Exits.*)

Heather *kneels by the grave to change the flowers.*

Janet   Am I that much of a disappointment to yu, Mum?

Heather   You had every chance he had.

Janet   Thass a laugh.

Heather   You threw it away.

Janet   So I wasn't as smart as Andy was, is that a crime?

Heather   I didn't raise my children to sit on their arses.

Janet   Oh man.

Heather   Wid a cup in their hands. You are more than what they tell you child.

Janet   Same old shit, all my life. Let me become what I wanna be.

Heather   A drifter.

Janet   My business.

Heather   What are you going to drift into next, Janet, after you and your boyfriend have run your restaurant into the ground?

Janet   Ryan! RY-AN. I swear to God, Mum, yer gonna say his name one day. Why yu want to see me fail?

Heather   Why do you? You were only sixteen, Janet.

Janet   Don't!

Heather   Sixteen! And you threw away your life. And for what? To get yourself a good fuck? An excuse for him to tell his friends, 'Yeah man, yu shoulda seen me bredren, yessir, I was givin' her sum serious portions.'

Janet *laughs*.

Heather   Yeah it's funny, Janet.

Janet   I don't think I've heard yu swear. Serious portions? Ryan weren't like that. We loved each other, we still do. Yu don't know us. I don't need yer acceptance no more.

Heather   Fine then, go home.

Janet   Yu go, I aint running from yu, it's wat Andy did.
Yu jus' wouldn't see how badly he needed to get away from
yu.

Heather   All I wanted wat was best for him.

Janet   Best for who though? Every day, man, yu were
pushin' him. Yu didn't raise a son, yu raised a
schizophrenic. He pretended he could handle everything yu
wanted for him, but inside he was crackin'.

Heather   Yu leave him alone, right?

Janet   Yu wanna know about him sneakin' into my
room . . .

Heather   Leave him!

Janet   . . . going through my drawers, readin' my diary,
thass how he knew I was pregnant, an' he couldn't wait to
tell yu, he didn't have the guts to front yu up about his
problems, so he took it out on me, ennit broth?

Heather   This child love to lie!

Janet   Mum, yu gotta listen to me, right? He was so
wound up, up for fighting anyone he was. Desperate to
prove to himself, jus' once, that he could be someone else.
Andy started the fight.

Heather   No.

Janet   I was there, Mum. I saw wat 'appened.

Heather   Wat yu mean yu saw? Yu said yu found him
lying there.

Janet   I know wat I said, I lied.

Heather   Oh God.

Janet   Everything that guy said in court was true, it was
self defence, Andy woulda killed Nicholls. He didn't know
who he was.

Heather   No. Child love to lie.

Janet   Mum let go of him. Jus' do it.

Heather   And then what?

Janet   Bloody hell! Did I always look wrong to yu? Was I born one minute and yu told the doctor 'Errgh, I don't want that, take it!' Is that how it was? Yu think I deserve it, yu don't think I hate myself?

Heather   Good. Yu should. Going on all the time about yu doin' nuttin wrong, that you didn't love to annoy me, going out wid that boy. (*Cuts in before* **Janet** *can.*) RY-AN! When you should have been at school. Andrew? So, is this the thanks I get? Andrew? Boy yu better answer me when I speak to yu! (*She waits.*) Yu nuh answer? Huh? Well you can go to hell boy. (*To* **Janet**.) Are you happy now?

Janet   No.

Heather   Child love to lie.

Janet   He knows yu don't mean it. He says he's standing next to yu.

Heather *moves away.*

Janet   Wat yu doin'? Ware yu goin'?

Heather   I'm lettin' go.

Janet   Yu don't want to say goodbye first?

Heather   If he's goin', he's goin', but tell him to go now. He gone yet?

Janet   I can't hear him.

Heather   He gone yet?

Janet   Yes.

Heather   Come let's go.

Janet   Mum?

Heather   Wat?

Janet   Wat about us?

Scene Ten

Outside **Bernice***'s house. Bernice is with* **Clarkey** *who is lifting her up in the air, swinging her around in the yard.*

Clarkey (*thrilled*)   Oh yes, yeah man!

Bernice   Yu want put mi down before yu hurt yer back!

Clarkey   Bernice! Yu love to give man hard time, yu nuh.

Bernice   I said yes.

Clarkey   Mi know, mi know. It were my mudda right, she dat mek yu 'fraid, right?

Bernice   Right.

Clarkey   All yu had to do were tell mi.

Bernice   Awright man.

Clarkey   Sorry, sorry. But yu nuh have to worry 'bout dat no more right. Yu go be de woman of de house, Mama go have to do wat yu say.

Bernice   She go obey mi?

Clarkey   Yes! And if she nuh like it, it too bad. And if dat son a' mine give yu trouble, yu tell mi and I go lick off 'im head. Wat kinda ring yu want?

Bernice   I don't mind. Long as it nuh cheap.

Clarkey   Mama say yu can wear her wedding dress.

Bernice   I nuh go wear her old dress.

Clarkey   It look nice Bernice, she tek care good care a' it.

Bernice   I don't care. I wan' be wearing a brand new dress from de shop, right? Yer mama dress! Yu best get dat money yu got hidin' under yer bed.

Clarkey   Shush.

Bernice   Clarkey! Yu don't really keep it under yer bed, man?

Clarkey   We go be happy.

Janet *comes out of the house, followed by* **Heather**.

Heather (*holding up a packet of tissues*)   You forgot these.

Janet   Cheers.

Heather   Don't want yu sneezing all the way home. You're going be late you know.

Clarkey   Hey Header, guess what . . .

Bernice   We bump into yer old boyfriend today, Georgie Taylor! 'Im tell us to say how'd yu do and 'im say 'im go come round soon.

Clarkey (*confused*)   Wa gwan?

Bernice   Yu go miss de plane.

Clarkey   Come Janet. (*Exits.*)

Janet *kisses* **Heather** *on the cheek, smiles.*

Heather   Wat?

Janet   Yu got my lipstick on yer cheek. Here.

Janet *uses one of her tissues to wipe the lipstick off* **Heather**'s *cheek.*

Heather   Call me when you get home, yeah?

Janet (*nods*)   Keep an eye on her for me, Auntie.

Heather   Keep an eye on me? You keep an eye on yourself, child.

Car horn beeps.

Janet   Laters. (*Exits.*)

Bernice   Alone at last, hey?

Heather   Fine. (*Hands her a letter.*)

Bernice   Wat dis?

Heather   Deeds to the house. It's yours.

Bernice   It's now yu realise?

Heather   Tek it nuh.

Bernice   No.

Heather   Wat yu mean, no?

Bernice   Mi mean no, mi nuh wan' it. Yu dat Daddy leave it to.

Heather   It's now yu realise? Take the house, Bernice.

Bernice   Mi nuh want it, Header.

Heather   I don't want it either.

Bernice   Too bad.

Heather   Well what are you going to do?

Bernice   Go live wid Clarkey.

Heather   Yu don't love him.

Bernice   Mi go marry him.

Heather   What?

Bernice   Yu deaf?

Heather   Yu mad!

Bernice   Yu say I should.

Heather   And it's now you start listening to me? Yu go marry a man yu don't love?

Bernice   'Im love mi. Dat'll do. Is why yu love to mek tings so complicated fer?

Heather   Never mind.

Bernice   Good, keep yer nose out.

Heather   So what do I do with the house?

Bernice   Leff it, burn it, I don't care any more!

Heather   Alright. (*Laughs.*)

Bernice   Wat yu laugh at?

Heather   Georgie Taylor? He's the one who had slick black hair, right? Wid 'im Tony Curtis look. 'Im drive a fancy car.

Bernice   An 'im have a fit behind.

Heather   Yes I remember him.

Bernice   Yu wan' drop by and say hello? Mi know ware 'im live.

Heather   No!

Bernice   Oh Header, don't be so . . . english!

Heather   No.

Bernice   Slip yu?

Heather *shakes her head.*

Bernice   Slip yu! (*Tags her, then runs off.*)

Heather   I'm not coming.

Bernice (*off*)   Come on, Header.

Heather *goes to run off stage, following after her sister. She feels a wind coming up behind her. She decides to make one last attempt.*

Heather   Son?

Bernice (*off*)   Header?

Heather *exits.*

Blackout.